HOT POPPIES

BOOKS BY LEON ROOKE

Novels

The Fall of Gravity, 2000
Who Goes There, 1998
A Good Baby, 1989
Shakespeare's Dog, 1983
The Magician in Love, 1981
Fat Woman, 1980

Stories

Painting the Dog, 2001
Oh! Twenty-seven Stories, 1997
Muffins, 1995
Who Do You Love?, 1992
The Happiness of Others, 1991
How I Saved the Province, 1989
A Bolt of White Cloth, 1984
Sing Me No Love Songs, I'll Say You No Prayers, 1984
The Birth Control King of the Upper Volta, 1982
Death Suite, 1981
Cry Evil, 1980
The Love Parlour, 1977
The Broad Back of the Angel, 1977
Last One Home Sleeps in the Yellow Bed, 1968

HOT POPPIES

LEON ROOKE

The Porcupine's Quill

Library and Archives Canada Cataloguing in Publication

Rooke, Leon
    Hot poppies/Leon Rooke.

Poems.
ISBN 0-88984-263-9

    I. Title.

PS8585.064H68 2005   C811'.54   C2005-900792-3

1   2   3   •   07   06   05

Published by The Porcupine's Quill
68 Main Street, Erin, Ontario NOB 1TO
www.sentex.net/~pql

Readied for the press by Anne Michaels; copy edited by Doris Cowan.
Typeset in Trump Medieval and Lithos, printed on Zephyr Antique laid,
and bound at the Porcupine's Quill Inc.

Represented in Canada by the Literary Press Group.
Trade orders are available from the University of Toronto Press.

We acknowledge the support of the Ontario Arts Council,
and the Canada Council for the Arts for our publishing program.
The financial support of the Government of Canada
through the Book Publishing Industry Development Program
is also gratefully acknowledged. Thanks, also, to the Government of Ontario
through the Ontario Media Development Corporation's
Ontario Book Initiative.

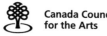

This book is for Russell Banks, who with a loose phrase dropped the poesy seed, for Tim Inkster who said 'Hustle it (the book) along to me', for the good people at Grano Restaurant who provided editorial shelter, and for Anne Michaels, fine *Hot Poppies* horticulturalist.

CONTENTS

There is no one like Rooke.
Take a look at this book!
He gets your attention
by hook and by crook.

— P. K. Page

EVERYTHING FROM HER MOUTH

1.

Everything from her mouth
I wrote down in a blue book.
I wrote down her eyelashes
her dreams and silences
when she slept. I did this
so many years
my fingers were glued
into the book.
Now you know me she said
and as she spoke a strong wind
came up and blew me I knew not
where. The book's pages scattered
into strange countries no one
had ever heard of.
Later
I learned women
in tropical fields planted
these pages in the earth and thus
the world came to know
cucumbers, radishes, even those red
new potatoes we're all so fond of.

2.

The women of the fields
sailed the seven oceans of
the green earth. They were
marooned on a thousand dark
isles where, with nothing else
to do, they discovered
they'd been impregnated by
the same dark man. The same
dark man had done the same
to their mothers in a distant time.
They felt this, and were horrified
by the absence of any hot proof
to bring before the authorities.
Destiny, the fate of our children,
were the words one heard. Coffee
prices plummeted, which led
to rioting among the natives
and a lot of loose talk that
we hear at night when sleep
is uneasy and our minds can only think
of fire drills which sounded at the most
unlikely hours and we were left
shivering in the school yards until higher-ups
determined we'd been punished
enough for one day.

3.

Carlos was the dark man's
name. But he had as many names
as the coffee bushes had beans.
He had sixteen names for each
hour in the day, and wore baggy suits
made from the earrings of every
woman he ever loved. The sun
had made him dark. His teeth
were pearls strung to whatever
length lips desired. He had
begun in clover, a horn
by each ear, which his women
clung to when lust whipped
their bones into other worlds.
He calls nightly to a blue dog
rumoured to exist though never
seen, yet the bowl every morning
emptied, always the blue face
in pans of bubbling water.

4.

Sometimes I wonder would
it have been better had I never
entered her words in the
blue book. I could have spent
my life far more profitably,
and bought myself lots of hats
and shoes and walked in the
rain any time the mood struck
me.

5.

Rain is upset. It has got its boots
wet. It fears it will come down
with something. It would seek shelter
if shelter did not provoke such
nightmares. He and the Missus have
had a spat. She follows the trade
winds: Mexico, the Caribbean. She's
only home to bicker.

THIRTEEN THEORIES
ON THE DEATH OF PRINCESS DI

1. Olive grower on Kos

My crop this year
Is the pride of the island.
It was her left foot
poking me in the night.

2. The tunnel builder in France

It is incomprehensible to me
that no one has mentioned
the blue dog.

3–13. From the *Oxford Companion to the Sorrows of Di*

A brilliant boy smitten by beauty
A love of the English countryside
So much at odds with the history
Of its governing bodies, the soft shoe
Performed by her on the Spanish Steps
One clear day in June, a duet sung beneath
Bruges apple trees while a blue dog
Haunched on the horizon, an orchard
Keeper who shot over their heads as
They ran naked though unknown woods,
The rhapsody of a smitten father, a hawk's
Feather found on the seashore at Nice
Placed for good luck in the heel of her
Left shoe, the cucumber slice on which
Were carved two hearts floating
In a blue martini, how they cried
'Faster, faster!' when
The brake line snapped.

JASPER JOHNS

Jasper Johns followed the trail
of the blue dog, coming at last
to a cave so low in a wall of caves
not even John Cage could stand up.
Mr Cage had issued a long-standing invitation
to one and all who found allurement
in following the blue dog's trail.
The hundred caves in the wall
were fully occupied by musicians
and painters and one poet who, frankly,
did not do that much. They held
communal dinners each evening,
performing acrobatic feats and
famous for the crooning of
an entire spangle of blue dogs. At
high tide all the caves filled with water.
It is not known where the artists went
at such moments (inspiration was
the assumption) or what the two Johns
did with themselves. They are not
an integral piece of the story.

DEAR BRITNEY

The limitations of which you accuse me
are considered small potatoes in my family,
which consists of the usual: aunts and uncles
and four chickens which have between
them one leg. I am not counting kissing cousins
or that lot living on the hill. I remember your
saying you could smell them coming. Warren
in Ohio was first to call and tell me my
limitations were no reason to annul the
marriage. I should see a priest, he said,
indicating to me he has gone over to the
Catholics or has been seeing them himself,
presumably over his own limitations, which
this family has grown old talking about.
Why did you take my watch? I left it by the
the whirl-eee-jig, but had every intention of
returning to pick it up before checkout time.
CNN, even that PBS guy with the drawl, asked
me were you a good husband. They didn't
dare ask what kind of wife I had been, knowing
I would sing the answer out hooting like Mahalia
(we live in such a dumb coffined-in world).
If you ask me, there was not a thing vulgar
about the ceremony or about anything else
we did . Life is made up of minutes, as I think
I told you, or as that songwriter woman in
L.A. told me. An eight-hour marriage is nothing
to be ashamed of and better than the forty years
of anybody else you know. I haven't mentioned
your imperfections to anyone except the
harbourmaster, who befriended me when
I occupied an interior state sealed off from
everything except fine drinking water. That
watch matters to me. I got it off a big shot,

just for showing him my teeth, which are
like pearls of wisdom cast across the whole
of your brain. Be sweet and keep the faith.
I know you will always love me. I
will be in Denver on the 10th. Ha.
I got that little 'th' right where I wanted it.

DENVER

A podge of nuns in Denver was auctioning off shoes
from their very own feet. Such dainty feet and each recently
pedicured. Come to my show, Britney told them. I want you sitting
right up front. I'll buy you an orphanage full of starving kids.
It's right that we all should live in this world without hindrance
to the stalwart initiative.

The shoes that night were strung by wire the length of the stage.
The nuns were enraptured. It was not themselves they saw walking.
They clapped heartily. The shoes were doing extraordinary
things they'd never done while on the nuns' feet. One Sister
wept. The inevitable, she was heard to say, is so long coming.
The other nuns shooshed her. Always there was a brainy Miss
spoiling the fun.

Britney interviewed applicants for the new orphanage. The line
stretched from Denver to the next town. She was wary. She wasn't
about to let bogus orphans occupy her beds. Her throat hummed a
quiet excitement. She imagined this must be how people used
to feel when contemplating a proposal of marriage to someone
they were sure had hidden flaws, such as insanity running in the
family. That long-ago day in the rain when her aunts discovered
her singing they had looked dreary as lampposts on a grey day.
You don't want to be thought of as callous, someone said. How
was she to know a dear uncle had died? It had struck her that
this deal could cost her pots of money. The barefoot boy before her
was tearful. I never said anything about buying these children shoes,
she told the nuns. I can't see why at least some of them couldn't
have brought their own silverware.

A BLEAK SITUATION

It was widely known among children
that there were twenty-seven Lassies,
often eight or nine in the same movie,
a stand-in taking the dangerous parts,
as when a child was rescued from a
flooding river. The children didn't mind
so long as Lassie alerted them to who
the bad man was. The Not-Lassie dogs
used to talk about this among themselves,
how to recognize who the bad man was
and how to slobber at the bad man's
sleeve without the real Lassie telling them
how disgusting the whole thing was. The
real Lassie's forte was to instill a bit
of class in what was otherwise a
bleak situation. Black Beauty,
as haughty a beast as ever drew
a horse's breath, said in *Variety*
that those dogs didn't know a good
flick from a pile of merde. Pigs will be
stars, if this keeps up.

PHENOMENOLOGISTS

Being is the unbeing being unspun
was how Heidegger saw the matter,
lacking his invitation to the meeting
in France. In the back of his mind
was a new ocean forming drop by drop
and knives dear Elfride sharpened
only yesterday.

CODA

Between the general
and the specific
I'll take the general.
You're excluded
because you're my honey.

POSTSCRIPT

John Cage said to his friend Jasper Johns, Lean on me.
Johns leaned. He said to the friend to his rear, Lean on me.
This request was passed on to those other artists who
had lived half their lives cursing rising tides. All those
calisthenics, those hobbled bones, all that sloshing water.
Lean on me. By nightfall a thousand leaning artists wove
like a long shoelace through the terrain. Why?
What were they up to?

AFTER-DINNER SPEECHES
AT (LORD) B.'S HOUSE

1. EASTER

It is Easter and our Lord awaits us. He speaks
censoriously of mother's table manners and wants
to know what ruffians are responsible for this
nonsense on our table. Since mother
turned vegan we have had to chase off our goats,
and turn other cheeks, including our Lord's.
Our Lord prefers to dine
in the dark closet beneath the stairs, where it so happens
my old dollhouse is stored. We look in from time to
time that we may remind ourselves what a person
should wear to the dining room and how a table
is properly set. Today it is noted that no one has
remembered to wheel in Aunt Roony
from the sickroom. Our Lord wants round-the-table
betting as to how precisely long she will cry out her eyes,
a stiff wager, none of that cheapskate business
such as shamed our palace at Christmastime.

2. DRIVEN ROUND THE BEND

M other was driven round it so often father said
she was the mosquito on a hot July night looking to
suck our blood. The sound was so much
in the ear we slapped ourselves silly,
which caused Aunt Roony to rise from a bed
of ashes to call the crisis line. In mistaken fury
she got hold of a foreign party and ambulances arrived one
by one to take us all away. Some of the family
have not been heard of since, little Julie, for instance,
my very own age, who had learned to walk on water
those hot July nights, though never to any announced
destination, in part because you cannot walk on water
and speak at the same time, or even afterwards address
your superiors, or, apparently, ever be seen again.

3. BALLAD OF THE APPLE TREES

Hearts have been left in San Francisco together
with Aunt Roony's mind. Prior to adventures of that ilk this
same mind had been scraped with one of those
instruments used for taking skin off potatoes
or carrots and burying them around apple trees
that are so strangely aloof to our natural laws and
less than respectful of their own.
Aunt Roony's lover, while in these trees, saw
himself as a sailor back from unknown lands
ruled over brutally by none other than Aunt Roony,
five feet two eyes of blue, though slim as the switchblade
so useful to a sailor skinning apples. Aunt Roony
buried five husbands but never succeeded in
burying her apple lover. It is his product we
see on our supermarket shelves, Aunt Roony's
Homemade Best Apple Pie, her old face on the box
lid looking up at a rakish sea-hopping lad high in
the apple boughs.

4. COME CLEAN

They wouldn't let me into America
          sticky fingers they said
from those French chocolates
sugaring my purse
foreign seeds between my teeth
my slouching they said was a dead
giveaway, shoes on the wrong feet.
They were no longer calling me sir.
'More lard in the gut might have fooled us,
hypnotism sometimes works,
proof of rightful birth
on allied domain might have won you
extended honeymoon on our soil
if I had not understood you to say
our spies sewed dead rats
in the hem of your coat
not to dwell on other weird shit
that rag holds inside your brain.'

5. UNHAPPY NEPHEW

Last Christmas when overwrought parents dropped
me off at this house for enjoyment of your revelry
I was presented with an umbrella, licorice sticks,
an exploding cigar, vials filled with water little Julie
was said to have walked upon. For my treks in the snow
I was given one seeing-eye dog and a picnic hamper
to see me through lost days. This year I have received
nothing and wonder what explains this waning
of your esteem for me.

6. THINKING OF YOU

I spend my every moment thinking of you, says
   an alien voice, which appears to arise withered from
an airless space beneath the house. Unconscionable!
roars dear father, and we pause
with forks at our lips to await how the alien voice
will respond. But there exists only soft whispering
followed by a prolonged spate of giggling,
until father's feet begin their usual drumming on the floor.
Time for sleep, he then says, and away he
goes, so heavy in the head chair our room tilts.

7. OUR ECONOMY

Of the onehundredtwentythousand jobs
added in July I got seventeen husband Jim
an even twelve fortyfive went to my pal
Sydney at the steamshipline shana got six
withouthardly trying Oshawa relatives
report a near hundred between themselves
my dog got one, cat two, the hamster in my
son's cage hustled parttimework at Sam's
Karwash and honey that's just in my
neighbourhood.

8. YOUR FACE

Your face is smiling at me out of what cause scarcely
could angels know. Your hands rove my body,
such liberties you take, sir, my father will want to
know your name, whence you came, in fact, the
very air your ancestors released. When we are
finished with this business you will forgive me if I
run away with your shoes.

9. LITTLE JULIE

Here's a tip of the glass to Little Julie invisible
still and yet walking on water, said to be enjoying
marital bliss these days while serving as a member
of Parliament in the far, far north. She was a fine
little runny-nosed girl and that we know this much about her
speaks very well of those among us who tenaciously
withhold all news of anything even vaguely touching
upon the unwise, the partial, the unimportant.

10. FLOWER

Oh the pretty flower on my night table that ran
all the way to my bedside from Singapore without taking
even the smallest sip of water.

11. LADY DEATH

S^{he}
     goes knocking why not
this door that door this one
is sweet also
I like the look
of the whole town here's
another inviting entry why
not stride right in but
(Oh I'm so tired) kerchoo
I must be coming down
with something it has been
a long day a long night is
that dawn I see glazing the hill
oops maybe tomorrow let me flit
that cat as I pass by
for the practice
you know look
at that cat run
I think I must need
a doctor.

12. LORD DEATH'S CHILDHOOD

I wanted to go to the dance
       but mother said I was too young
four I was four I think she said I was
four which was much too young she said
so I must have been four she wurra wee darkish-
featured pelly wiz ma mither she wiz gaein' oot doll'd
ope each night blap there gaes the cat I wiz a mere wee wean
four year auld she could hiv covurred that cat wit a sheet or sump'tin
I could see them dancing across the field a thick haar it wiz.
Four hundred of them dancers some I counted twice I
was clever and could go up to a thousand using my
tables they were my own tables I didn't need
anyone's permission later on I went
to a dance my first dance I took myself
I was able I wiz awl scented
and doll'd ope like a
wizard in the mood for a good
time blap there gaes the cat I want you
to know I covurred that cat wit a sheet or sump'tin
then I called mother across the field I hollered mother will ye dance
wit me she wurra wee doll'd-ope pelly who come running fast the whole
night I floated
                    on her shoes
                              it was sensational.

13. NURTURING THE PRETTY

It's Autumn
   and here come the women
to witch
us leaves
back to trees.
Madame,
please!

14. FATHER WHO ART

Oh prince of peace in whom I trust
   you took my springtime and left me dust
         You got me too early
      Sincerely,
      Your Shirley

15. FORGET LAWYERS

Personally
    I personally
Do not admit
To any debts
Obligations
Promises
Enlistments
Or commitments
Of any variety
Incurred in my name
Or in any
Sundry name
Attached to mine
Bone-blood or
Otherwise
With exception
Of the full medley
Of expenses
Covenants
Concordats
& other such deals
Struck under full moon
Past midnight
While in the soup
& meanly relevant to
The forty-seven households
Situated on Barden
And York Streets
(But not the Smiths),
My town.

16. THIS MAN CORTAZAR

I mean to clear up in the minutes left me, and for the final time, any lingering disquiet you may have regarding the brief chronicle entitled 'The Lines of the Hand', by this man Cortazar. It should be clear by this hour that matters did not unfold as the author tells us they did. Your naive acceptance of the contrary, has, as you are aware, often left me speechless and if I have banged on pots and pans through many dark nights and wallowed in snow in my long underwear you now know the cause. You will recall that in the very first sentence of this tale comprising scarcely half a page this man Cortazar dramatically affirms the tossing of a letter onto a pine table, the leaping of a single line from that letter, the line's descent along a table leg to the parquet floor, up a wall and through a painting to the roof of the house. We need say little more, I hope, about the identity of the party who so cavalierly tosses a letter onto the table. For reasons that elude me, my wife presumes the party in question is female. We know what rogues men can be and the letter-writer can be forgiven for wanting to have her bath, dress, and for once go out to dinner with a quiet haberdasher who will not make nasty scenes or fail to admire her ankles. It has taken some brow-beating of the steamship company to have her goods retrieved from the boat you will presently hear about, but this irritating task has been accomplished to the envy of everyone. Let the brute sulk, it will do him good, for what man was ever of any worth until first he has been made to walk on nails. The woman can afford, in her letter, to throw a kiss to the man you will presently hear more about, kisses being so much ingrained in a woman's nature in one form or another they brazenly fly through even the thinnest air. Let the brute make of this kiss what he will. All the same, it has upset her, this line's leaping from the page, when it knew she had no intention of posting the thing, or posting it to Bora Bora, where the boat might or might not be docking a week or two hence. Language has no business behaving like this, and she will give up French, or burn this letter, if another word dares to escape her lovely page.

N ow back to the scheming of this runaway line. I need not, I trust, pursue every detail of the line's subsequent movement, fascinating though many of you believe these details to be. Suffice it to say that the line escaped to the roof of the letter-writer's house, arriving in the street by way of the aluminum cable of a lightning rod. It is true that this man Cortazar does not tell us the cable was aluminum, nor in fact does he call it a cable. It is called a chain in this man Cortazar's brief, though if you want to continue to think of it as a chain then you may hereafter decant your own champagne and in no glass of mine, for I will not drink with you however closely we may be related by marriage, blood, chemistry of friendship, or the waddling ions of infinity.

W hatever the case, the line temporarily becomes lost from our eyes in thick street traffic, though soon enough it is to be seen climbing the stocking leg of a pretty woman aboard a bus, although the pretty woman holds no essential importance to this man Cortazar's tale, however much certain scholars at our table wish to pretend otherwise. The bus deposits our line at a docking area familiar to any who reside in port cities or have had the misfortune of visiting same. The line next 'zigzags', 'slopes' and 'wriggles'
        (excuse, please, a drink of water)
its way through 'hostile territory' ruled over by customs officials only earning their daily bread. Seen only by rats, by one means and another the line boards a docked vessel of the ocean-going variety; it is next found crossing the first-class deck of this vessel 'whose turbines give off an agreeable sound'. Here the main hatchway provides some difficulty for our line, this man Cortazar hastily tells us, yet it perseveres and in the alleged tale's conclusion, so we are informed, the line negotiates its entry into (here I quote the entirety) 'a cabin where an unhappy man is drinking cognac and listening to the hooting of the stack indicating departure, climbs the seams of his trousers, past the knitted vest, slips back as far as the elbow, and

with a final burst of energy, takes refuge in the palm of his right hand just at that moment when it begins to close around the handle of a revolver'.

Our dear mother attests that surely such an ending can only mean that the unhappy man has now put aside his revolver, having been moved to new and nearly incomprehensible levels of hope by the tender charity of the line in question. She will even tell you that she knows what this line is, and furthermore contents herself with the belief that in future all will be 'peaches and cream' for this pair, if I may quote her, which I feel compelled to do given the frequency with which I have heard her screech out this absurd cliché through the many dark nights I rolled in my underwear in the snow, to the delight of some many of our neighbours and the dismay of that new pair living to our immediate right, those damnable Gideons, formerly of Bora Bora, romantic icons I yearn to hear no more about.

AS TOLD TO ANONYMOUS

My life as the sister you saw disguised as a woman
Fated to end up shipwrecked in an angry sea.

by P.K. Stagecraft (as told to Anonymous)

1. SISTER FRANNY: PHOTO ALBUM

do I look a little plump to you?

here is the loveless boy

all of us sisters loved
the loveless boy

we plagued with love's arrows
  the loveless boy

even so he remained
a luckless boy

that woman in the background's the mother of
the loveless boy

now isn't that strange here again is
the loveless boy

We all loved
  the loveless boy
we took turns smooching him
even mother did
we called ourselves his girls.

ex
    cuse
    me
    tell me again
    your name?

that dog
I believe needs to go to the bathroom.

2. SISTER BOO BOO

Up yours Mac was not a thing I normally
said in public but if you work your ass off
surely a wee bad mouth can be forgiven
            eh girls
bloody the nose I say
            just for laffs ya know
piss and fuck ya know
words of that ilk to uphold
the kingdom's butter
is that a radish between my lips
no honey that's me smiling
            at ya mother
            ya mother tongue
cut yaself
            why not shoot
yaself
            in the brain
            set yaself ablaze
fall yaself under a tired mule
let it kick you to death
            ya fat sludge
            ya fat goofball
            ya fag ya fruit
did you think I was talking sign language here?

is that ya dog

does it come when ya call

let's show some class, boys.

3. HAPPY BIRTHDAY, SISTER SALLY

Slack Sally in goose-slick pearls
went to church on Sunday
stayed the full day, came back to
her man on the eve of another birthday,
plucked cards from the mail slot,
sat down to a beer and a smoke, pushed
off her shoes, slid low as a weasel
in short grass, let go with a hacking cough,
took a quick peek at the cards,
looked her old shit full in the eye,
thinking of her mother dead and gone
but sitting here slag-heaped
in this same chair the same room
the same old shit with his same rummy eyes
looking back at her, back all the way,
thinking she'll say to him, I got
a sister sits on the Supreme Court,
I got another says in the card here,
Would we like us a dog.

Would we?

But wanting first
to ponder the issue herself.

The jack of it being who is it gets in
the first word first. It's like that these days
here with ya shoes off, ya smoke,
ya drink, ya birthday cards: ya got
to have ya wits about ya
when you come home.
Relax a minute and its some other jasper
laying down the laws, him getting in there

this time, the fat turd, the old lardbucket,
him intoning in his most royal of tongues,

  Sally, ya know, Sally, ya needs more religion
in ya life, ya eyes all lit, ya face shiny,
religion becomes ya is what I'm saying,
old gal.

4. WHAT'S COOKING, SWEETHEART?

Flat-top boats
docked in pier three:
If each day one woman
more less brings onto
the deck one rock
more less how many will be
the years before
Cap'n Jack remarks
upon the pile at his feet
or sees yet again
his wife arriving
with yet another rock
perhaps the final one
yes we could say that's why
she's so often up
during the night
these rocks sinking
every boat the women
there under cold moons
plotting sabotage
of seagoing vessels
what a woman must do
these days for a man
to notice any
sourness in marriage.

5. SHOOT A FAWN, WHY NOT

As John Said said to Mary
John Said said to Mary,
honey, if you've ever
given thought to our
good name what
we most have going
for us is the child
in your beautiful
belly.

To which Mary Said
said, John, dearest, your
words how they thrill
my ears I can see
that child now
in his birthday suit
standing on a chair
watching us grill
this fish on
a good-as-new stove
To which John Said said,
Mary love do you think
the time has come
to turn
this
fish?

6. MAY A SISTER APPROACH THE BENCH?

Nice is for the nice gale
that swept me to you
me to hear you sing
and me to say nice things
to say all the things that nice is
for instance Nice (Niece, slowly)
which is nice enough
if you know how to live
employed I mean and occupying
a nice sea abode with nice sea breezes
Nice (slowly) as synonym for pleasant
which is close enough to nice 'n' easy
to be sheer joy me in bikini
you in ya birthday suit Nice
will bring you nice things
I'd ask for more if it existed
but do not intend taxing myself
in Nice-by-the sea
   our once loveless boy
   here nicely loving me.

7. EARTHQUAKE IN PERUVIAN MOUNTAINS NEAR ERSQUAG

Minor quakes, tremors, no more than five
seconds occurring at sundry intervals
daily through the past seven hundred years,
the earth never still, no deaths yet
recorded, what the locals speak of as
quivers meant to keep the blood perking,
shakes meant to let others know whereof
we speak. Not a single disadvantage
save that one day each year we must set our clocks
forward 1,500 seconds, let's say
an even thirty-five minutes, for all that lost time
shaking.

Bring the dog, bring boy/girlfriends
bring lucky loveless boy
come soonest, singing.

> Love ya (you),
> ya sister (your) Stagecraft
> all shook up in Ersquag

EVERYTHING ABOUT MANY, LESS ABOUT YOU

CONTINUATION OF THE JAMES TATE POEM 'PEGGY IN THE TWILIGHT'

After the host said to me he had no one at the party
by that name, I curled up under the blanket with her
and passed the night exactly as one is told to do
in the manuals. In the morning I asked the host
and his mistress if I and Peggy might trouble them
for breakfast. A spot of toast and juice would be fine,
I said, Peggy and I would be grateful. The mistress,
whose name I never got, said they were having Harvey
Walbangers. My host said, 'You are worrying me. Who
is this woman you keep calling Peggy?'
But I saw Peggy at that moment fly out the door,
and instantly dropped all pretence of civility, and ran
after her, because love only comes once to those in my line
and I wanted it badly.

TIDES AND CURRENTS IN THEIR FLUX

Allrightyright, loosen up, pay attention,
we have the two-year-old Freud, we got
the Jones guy, Ernest, with the Freud biography,
we got Leon Edel, the James guy, calling
to task the Jones guy, by no means
forget other attendant parties —
Freud's parents, various sightseers
in town for what they can get out of it,
mostly we got the two-year-old Freud's
baby brother catapulting from between
the mother's legs, that's where Freud's curse is
says the biography guy, Jones, git off of it says Edel,
that's rot and you know it, Edel complaining
that at age two not even a bright screw like Freud
is likely to surmise someone other than him
knows mother more intimately than he knows her,
faint chance, says Edel, even if little Freud is familiar
with how families do things and get things done
he's not going to suspect his 'fine and perfect' father
is on intimate terms with this clumsy business.
But listen up, even Edel must admit young Freud
was alert to the moans and groans, the howls
and shrieks, he's a little hellion is young Freud
since he learned to walk, into everything and all over
every home inch you can name. I tell you, the boy
is up there with García Márquez who only last
week let it be known that at this same age he was already
changing his own diapers and running to the store for bread,
even signing mortgages on the house. So I am for one am
taking this Edel's criticism of this Jones guy with a grain of salt,
I am unswayed by his argument that further along and become the genius
        we revere, our man
Freud could have looked back in a reflective mode,
say on a sweltering Saturday night when not much

was doing at the clinic, patients off catching
zees, staff out playing tag on the lawn,
Doctor Freud might not have thought um,
my brother's birth, um, not much
I liked about that, um, someone more intimate
with Mother than I was, um, a definite possibility,
I believe I can rule out anything accidental about this
affair, ummm, dare I cast a suspicious eye upon
'dear and perfect' papa, um, must look into this,
how I wish at least one in the compound had
had the foresight to at least
                              chew up a wedge
                              of gum
                              plug up
                              the goddamn keyhole.

Source: Leon Edel's lecture, 'The Biographer and Psycho-Analysis', read at the
Edward Hitschmann Memorial Meeting, Boston Psychoanalytic Society and
Institute, March 23, 1960.

BRITNEY AMONG THE SQUIRRELS

Make no mistake about it in our neighbourhood
we are at war with the squirrels, the black, the grey,
Each hefty as a flying raccoon, smack them in the face
and how quickly the cheek turns. In the night they enter my bed
they say we like you better in the nude it's so much nicer
having a relationship with people who are pleasant
don't youo find? Yesterday in my Britney rubadub bath
a trio of old-timers of infinite capacity, of the ———— variety
(that's a blank, buddy) said they would wash my back,
small comfort in loose-living times of infinite stress was
my verily thought. Any-the-hoo, they soaped me past the thighs
of consciousness, washed my hair with unknown essences
flown in from Peeking and pilfered from drugstore shelves,
product of Esso in association with Dow Laboratories
the old Ipana School of Worshipful enigma now enjoying vogue
among the squirrel set. You look smashing, they said,
looks like yours could power submarines, fuel SUVs, fuel
interstellar warfare if the country ever got itself
in a true mess, oh Bushie, I thunk, please call me.
Following a time-out ('Ermine does nothing for you, honey')
was dinner with other show-stoppers at the Precious Few.
Later on I went out with a quite good-looking girlie
to a phooshe or fooshi or whatever was in olden days a rave,
the paparazzi caught us coming home and we were
in all the papers stoned but not so you could tell it
no mention made of the several drive-by shootings.
Squirrels of the ———— variety (that's a blank, buddy)
read the reports to us over late breakfast, those squirrels
will do anything to get a toehold in hot society,
only the next day, eating birdseed off my silver spoon,
remembering to tell me oh yeah your mother called,
she did.not.leave.a number.

Sleepy-time on the yacht out from Port-au-Prince,
somebody's wedding, my lady vents:
'Those are not squirrels, man.'

BREASTS

how when you fan the pages the breasts word
flies out like geese going south
flash any book at random
juvenilia editions
for little goats, treatises on the atom,
last night I was deep
into an algebra assignment
wind riffled the pages and here was an entire
text given over to the breasts word,
on the street that very minute
six of the very things themselves
breasts abreast of breasts,
enchantment walked bright circles
around my eyes
someone inside my ear said
great god there he goes again
with that breasts business
a contagion has struck
this household.

ROPE WALKING

Horses and riders at the end of a rope
stretch it tight boys I mean to walk that thing

so I came to Rome sufficiently venerated
to stroll the old city without chaperone

at the holy maze that is St. Peter I was lost
with a sore neck until closing time

come evening I took time off to see the Pope
had trimmed his nails he said he'd missed me

same here Dad I came home on a good tailwind
the good woman fed me her meatloaf when

it comes to culinary arts she's a woman second to none
though something of a let-down the whole show was

both horsemen asleep in the saddle
horses showing not a drop of sweat
my best rope dragging the mud

hardly my idea of how to work a crowd.

TIME AND NO MAN

The Heretofore and the Hereafter
having a powwow
agreed upon a compromise
which would affect all
it would need lawyers
and I was a lawyer so
I rolled up my sleeves.
Scribes, underlings, of both parties
zipped in and out,
all in good blue suits,
some quite brazen
others like squished toothpaste tubes,
I'm happy to say
I grooved with both sides.
'That'll do it for today,'
Heretofore in the end said
Hereafter let venture
a quiet rut of obscenity
not yet in the public record
and possibly never to be,
but safely in my briefcase
I think I can assure
you of that simple truth.

CHENEY/BUSH ROTTWEILER TEAM

'It is common knowledge that a cat left alone
in a house will go crazy from all those bad things
house plants say to it, and those little scratchings
within your walls are not nice mice merely amusing themselves.
In addition our sources reveal a cat is predetermined in its genes
to go haywire when left alone, plus there is all the lingering
disquiet, let's say outright animosity, a cat has
for all your previous, not to mention present,
alliances, lovers, parents and friends.
So your choice is either
give up those dalliances
or quit your job and stay home,
or pay us to exterminate
the beast.'

BIBLICAL TALE

I who have carried this cross
for so many years am damned tired
of crows using it as roosting post,
not to mention the wild birds'
shit in my mouth.

HOW WE ELECT OUR PRESIDENT

After what happened with the Empire down in Florida we gave up trying. Now we send out secret ballots to about one hundred and sixty top countries and the nominee scoring highest, to put it simply, he's in. Some years back the same candidate was nominated by three nations. We called that Ruling by Landslide. At the moment we are led by a seven-year-old boy. Our economy is brisk, no one lacks for much that is necessary. The usual crew is making the usual call for change, but not even they dare fuck with our constitution. It's inviolate, which is to say, written in stone, which is precisely how we like it. Are things bad where you are? Do you feel disgraced? Then book a cruise. We're a hot-blooded, family first, party-all-night people, but for those wanting tranquility, pace befitting the single eye, we've got desert isles, ski slopes, golf, anti-tipping you're the boss laws. Next year we get our UN veto vote. Then, look out.

FORSOOTH, YOU CANNOT

No, you cannot, nor could I, nor could any other
although the orchid man, wearing a houndstooth suit,
matching hat, socks and shoes, together with a matching brother,
did, or said they did, as did my old stunner girlfriend Peggy,
her sister, the full family excluding cousins. The president
did, and by God you'd think if a Bush of that tribe did
then anyone could, but anyone cannot, as you have
now been informed many times over. It was
never true that pensioners and hat-check
girls could. They cannot. I repeat,
they cannot. Stay home. Tithe daily. Pay your rent
on time and forget hat-check girls, however alluring.

In total, less than a dozen did, though most only partially,
then only at midnight, and only at a certain midnight,
walking backwards, carrying orchids (somersaulting
proved no advantage), some wearing
clothing of specific houndstooth design,
accessories, too, never mind their
being a bitch to drag.

All others cannot, may not, and
had better not try. You
are being watched,
you know. We
have your
number.

In the meantime, our office remains open to serve you,
nine till three weekdays, otherwise by private arrangement.

MAHALIA

Mahalia Jackson is so pissed off
she didn't get to heaven she's
booked herself nightly at
the Leaky Spigots dive
on Jarvis Street. The others
didn't
get there
either but don't
think they are letting it
get them down. Glory beckons
in all directions and, same as always,
these chil'ren out in the audience
don' know nuthin'. Not even nada.

DON'T CALL ME

We called the mover
to move
and the mover
called the caller
to tell us
he was not moving
now or ever
and if we valued
our lives
we would be well advised
to stay exactly
where we were
and that includes, he said,
any further use
of the telephone.

CONTINUATION OF THE JAMES TATE POEM 'THE CONDEMNED MAN'

The warden dropped by the condemned man's cell
for their usual conversation. 'What's new?' the condemned man
asked, and the warden told him of Hurricane Frances, which
at that moment was uprooting Florida. 'Second scrape in three weeks,'
said the warden, 'though don't worry about Florida, those Bush
brothers are on the job.' The condemned man, who at that moment
was dining, asked how this business of a final Death Row dinner
got hatched. 'It seems unnatural,' he said, 'even to be thinking
about eating.' The warden admitted it was a somewhat odd practice,
and rarely worked well in Florida or Texas, and in fact a pig farmer
over in Dalalia had state contracts to pick up the leftovers.

MARTHA STEWART LIVING

A man at the Dominion was looking long and hard
at chicken breasts, first at economy trays
then at smaller portions, finally hefting the smaller
and saying to the woman nudging his rear, 'Do you suppose
these are free-range chickens?' The woman shouldered
him aside. She was in a hurry, she said, and in no mood
for asinine chit-chat. 'But no,' she said, scurrying away,
'I don't suppose those are free-range. I suppose those
are dead chickens.' At which point, or actually about thirty
seconds later, the man said to me, 'Some days I am happy
I never married.'

PERFECT IN HIS SMALL WAY

Now here was a woman
who could see
clear through her man
to the stone wall
inside him. On that wall
stood another man
his feet on fire
shouting perfect words
at ugly strangers.

BELL AND BROOM

I was having a few at the Paddock Lounge
on Bathurst when I got to remembering
the inmates of the Asylum
down on Sparke Street
during a time when I was young,
free, and brave. I spoke of this to
the two beautiful Lauras,
it being a moment of respite
for the Paddock Lauras who sat
on stools either side of the stool
I sat upon.

I believe some time may have elapsed.

It is thus possible that I laboured to depict
in the two Lauras' minds the exact city block
the Asylum sat upon, and how in late summer
black twig arms twisted between asylum bars
to reach pecans on the tree in my yard.

'Those crazy people are stealing our pecans'
was my precise charge to parental objects in
for a quick wash, if the day chanced to be a Friday.

'Top us up, Jack,' the two Lauras said.

One day the entire structure goes boom,
no one telling those lunatics their one earth's
habitat was under the wrecker's ball. You tell insane
people such news they are apt to go ape. Who knows the rampage
to ensue? So it is as I inform the two Lauras — exit doors
propped open, arrows painted on walls —
that way to freedom, dear.

The entire furtive bunch escaping the sunrise boom.
What credence to give rumours of cattle prods,
of women shoved into snowbanks attired in
flimsy negligees?

What I want to know of the two Lauras
is where this gang got to. Did one or two live
happy lives? But the two Lauras have gone on a long walk
on their private heaths. This Paddock crowd's
a nicely groomed, festive lot. Skinny nighthawkers
heat the long rail. You can't tell, looking,
that they come from where I and the two Lauras
know at least some of them
come from.

BLIND MAN REQUIRES WHIRLWIND

'Ya need to be with people
when ya honey dies,' my honey said,
'Ya need the ache of the human voice,
ya need to feel the weight of a woman's
brain in ya seatpants.' Forty long days
I been riding Greyhound, took
Via Rail Toronto Chicago,
six weeks I substitute-drove
Catawauga County's lil' chil'ren's
school bus, I sat in with them
singing songs, drawing frogs,
boxy crayon houses smoke
pouring from the chimney,
I frequented five-hour baseball games
for the sheer luxury of a seventh-inning
stretch, one long year I've measured
the unsolid wealth of cheers and groans,
even so, remorse slithers on my tongue
like withering bone, I'm damp with shock
at my lifelong honey stealing off
to outspeak death through quiet sleep.

BRITNEY REVISITED

Britney shifts into high gear
with the driest Dri Gel ever
she's super moisturized by the skin's
own Serine & Alanine
she's pumping hell for leather
a genuine road warrior
specially highlighted front
and rear *My jetliner Little Dipper*
assyou ask me why
that Jackson babe only showed
one breast, honey the answer's obvious,
look at my two I got nipples
you'd swear cut cleaner than the sword
of Damocles I got multi-tonal highs and lows,
got the best of the vegetable kingdom
I'm sky-high amped Global Earth girl
men have melted for a lot less
take that Helen woman
the earth falling for a squeaky voice
her strength all in her feet, fat-necked rosy-cheeked
purveyor parlayer of the goods, whatever the case,
whip that lariat, hogtie the dreck,
when I'm finished with you
you'll be dead dick
at the bottom of the pool,
Britney woman's cozy with your fantasies,
she feeds your heart
through sausage tubes,
your organs are the nourishing primer
lifting and lengthening her eyelash days
honey don't ya know
I'm blessed with the bliss of maturity
plus plunging off high cliffs
from the vitality of the freshness

of youth I'm stealing your orgasms
for my own self, I got the cleavage
of soccer balls, 'because you're worth it,'
that's my motto, I'm sellin' my dazzling plumping lip thing
utilizing hip-hop micro-crystal breakthru technology
I'm 99 percent oiled top to bottom,
sleek satin in Satan's Ballroom
God's skin never lets me down
I'm divinely incarnate, volumized,
turbo-brushed, the original clean sweep
my nutritional pores rich in the anima acids
sisters in the dark, you plebes to
the workhouse don't be a darkie
down Cottonpick Lane, take my advice
and enhance your blush never be plain again
you'll discover your secret powers
honey lip-synch these words
you want your wood chopped
then wax those hairs
the competition's washed out,
they got a faded mind-set,
these poppies lack
the good colour retention
    what I'm saying is,
            girls,
        Britney's human,
           and has human needs
              the same as me,
                    though different from you.

MY BRIDE

My bride
comes with fruit
fruit trees, shrubs, herbs
an entire savannah strapped
to her back.

How softly the rain falls.

Look how slowly she advances along the road.
One more river to cross
and this young beauty
will be

an old woman

(did wind shriek? did our parrot 'Ritz'
truly fly from Buenos Aires in three days?)

closing the door

(did the dog 'Blue', flung three miles
by lightning bolts, drag herself home
on three legs?)

on fifty years

(the precise time, please,
before a favourite dress disintegrates ...)

of gruelling

(in the wash?)

      marriage.

THE WOMEN'S DISPENSARY

New arm?
Your left eye?
It's hard out there,
no easier in here.
Rapid turnover.
Today my counter girl
called in sick,
a kidney punch.
The supervisor's
hospitalized,
Nerves, I'm told.
We're tough, though.
No porcelain dolls
in this camp....
We walk on water,
fly on ice, even
on down days.
We get a flood of calls
through late night hours:
hang-ups. breathing. pizza requests.
'Are you the Escort Girls?'
We get, 'Hello? Hello?
Are you there?'
We are always here.
We have three hundred offices
throughout the province. None
west of _____, none east of
_____. You fill in the blanks.
Our funding comes from
the Mystic Arts. Silent
Auctions. Barbecues.
We don't do layaway.
We don't let you run a tab.
Tattooing is next door.
Hello? Hello? Are you there?

ANNUAL LETTER TO THE MISSING WIFE

Oh honey come home.
The sod you walked on I've fertilized
until it's smooth as Kentucky bluegrass.
Your lipsticks I've mounted under glass.
Now the New Guggenheim wants them.
Sotheby's auctioned off the Elvis velvets,
we got top dollar.

I've taken down walls.

By the way, and I am so sorry for this,
I got your password and am privy
to your emails. Funny to me how
you never mention my name.

At dinner this Sunday last your parents
looked at your empty chair with blank eyes.
They bespoke enthusiasm for the improvements
I've made. We watched election returns
on the new TV. No one spoke for twenty
minutes. We barely had oomph to put on shoes.

Your chickadee died. Truth is a cat got her,
not our own cat J-Lo but Condoleezza's ugly beast
of a tom next door.

We are bringing a class action
suit against those Rice girls.

By the way, the paternity case brought by
your sister is dead in the water.

We are wondering how you are liking Iran.
Why you'd give up one ayatollah for another
is something your friends can't understand.
The feeling here is that you never understood
freedom. Concepts like the one true religion,
a nation one under God, were but a faint breeze under your nose.

No matter what the VP says we can't believe
you're a covert agent for the CIA
I remember all the times during our cocktail hours
you said Fuck the CIA. Often we toast
you with those words.

You may not have heard your daughter Beth's
now lead singer in the Country-Gone-Mad
percussion ensemble. They took Saskatchewan by storm
and a world-wide Green Earth tour definitely
is in the picture. I'd send you the CD if I knew where.
She's got the idea others have been using your identity
or it wasn't you who was here in the first place, a
stand-in Mom.

Baby Clyte was thirteen yesterday.
She looks at the roof dish with the same curled
lip you had for it when CNN and that Fox bunch
brought in our news of the world from the panoramic
dungeons of the Saved Again.

My desk overflows with all the sheets I've got on you
through the Freedom of Information Act. I'm devoting
my entire life to this project, though it makes me
a poor man. You'll recall the song: I think
I'll dust my broom.

I miss you and love you with the terrible love
of a pilgrim caught at the diabolical crossroads
history has strummed.

Sky remains indispensable
though weird shit
floats upside-down within it.

MEMO ON MOVING UP (OR DOWN) IN THE WORLD

Go in the most obliging direction.
Tell your friends of developing plans.
Acquire a satchel. Fold a shirt inside.
Under your arm carry a pillow for comfort
through the first long night.
This will get you through the hardest part.
Piety is advantageous. Grapefruit is restful
to the eyes. Police in unmarked cars
will offer assistance. Refuse politely.

SEX

how bodies
have need afterwards of rearranging themselves
how old lovers hug the back gate
how the gate
swings back and forth in such sultry air
how crapshooters swarm the dark lanes

'Come to daddy, oh mama be good!'

how your mind
allows you to enter a lighted room,
sit at a table,
and calmly brush your hair.

DEBONAIR INSOMNIACS

Select billionaires of the administration
held a dance in Fallujah, their planes having strayed
from the planned destination because of flaws in Crusade maps.
Angels came down from the head of a pin in fond embrace of them.
A Saudi prince sold used shoes on the street, as was
his summertime custom. At a high window
a bijou heroine lost her courage at the last minute.
Last minutes are not trustworthy the way old friends
sometimes are. Air gets upset when you try kissing its lips
when air is in the mood for something totally private.
An electrician in St. Petersburg is thinking about salted peanuts.
His daughter sprinkles salt on her toenails. The thought
of orange segments on a pretty plate gets me
through the night. I'm not promising this
will assist you. My sister's one
it didn't.

EVERYTHING ABOUT MANY,
LESS ABOUT YOU

I know everything about many, less about you.
Are your doors locked against thieves?
Do you have a dog?
What did you eat last night and was it good?
When did you last cry in the rain?
If I stole your heart
what ransom would you pay?
How quickly?

NOTE FOUND PINNED TO THE BODY
IN A BROTHEL BED IN A VILLAGE
IN THE SOUTH OF FRANCE

Dear good friend,
I try all day to ride the Faulkner ponies
and in the evening attend the brothels.
Fish are thrown through windows, orphans seen running.
The ponies see me coming and race headlong into each other.
They go through steel walls.
                    All night I wait in a brothel bed for someone to come.
Headless little men
            pivot on shiny heels by the doorway. The ponies disavow me.
We endure maudlin scenes on street corners involving police officers
from icy slopes. The Colet woman, trim ankles under chestnut hair
sculpted as a mountain range claims
affection for me.
I have yet to ...

to discern
the beautiful breasts Gustave
wrote so bravely about. Brothel girls bemoan
their 'punctured tambourines'.
                    Yesterday on the village green a black bear
joined us for tea. Such a merry fellow. Talk in the brothels is of politics.
They could be a learned race if people like you and me only left them
alone. Face creams and science texts are adored equally. Faulkner
ponies pound the boulevard night and day, seeking entry into hell.
Babinet, a charwoman of lemon scent, laughs at me alone in my bed.
She has heavy opinions on war and inevitably proves herself
knowledgeable of assassinations and executions
planned for dawn.

A court magistrate declares the Supreme Being does not intend me
to ride Faulkner ponies. Children are astride these beasts every noon.
Girls in sunbonnets gallop three and four abreast: sleep's sheep etch

my lavender walls. Colet's limbs are a daily torment. She thinks ill of me. I hate her poems with the wistful longing of dear Gustave. Sheeted women fly by my open door; shrieking phantoms in exit from ruined worlds. Faulkner ponies shun all rest. They and orphans and headless men rule the streets. Mine is the lone reasonable voice in this country. Babinet who knows everything laments the sex drive of insects, so powerful they burrow through walls. I will die someone's unknown son, likely to ... to ...

night

LIFE OF A PROGRESSIVE PARTY CIVIL SERVANT
CALLED OUT OF RETIREMENT
IN BENEFIT OF A BUSY NATION

They housed me with seven others in a room close by the police station,
twice each day I was to report to the Captain,
three times each afternoon and evening to a higher authority,
while sleeping my passage was monitored by officials expert
in the task, five times each day I was compelled to face the East
in prayer, on Saturdays the Synagogue of the First Light beckoned,
on Sundays I was free to take my knees to Catholic, Lutheran,
or Jehovah's Witnesses houses, if I failed to arrive at any
of these places at the appointed hour I was to be hunted down
and shot, shot quickly through the heart, I was in fact shot
three times on the Monday, twice on the Friday, hanging,
I was told, was not out of the question. In the meantime,
I was to work ('No wages for the likes of you'), my workday,
if you please, began at 6:00 a.m., ended at midnight, then I must
walk the President's dog, not to mention soap one hundred doorways
daily (the Remonstiv area), tend neighborhood gardens (the
Deplovnovic compound), keep up my lessons at correspondence school,
sew and mend uniforms retrieved from our dead soldiers at the front,
polish the Captain's sedan, groom the horses of those higher
authorities, proselytize along with my Jehovah's Witnesses
brothers and sisters each and every Thursday, feed the fish
in the Archbishop's pond, wind the city clocks,
control an outbreak of lizards up by Union Station,
in fact perform another one thousand deeds not reported upon here
(paper is scarce), yet even so I want it to be known
that I was never so busy, so fatigued, so worn down to the bone
that I did not find time for love.

ORPHANED BY CIRCUMSTANCE

AND NOTHING BUT

I so wanted leave of truth
that when the invitation
arrived from hell
I went with the speed of light
and sat at the devil's table
for a seven-course dinner.
Wine was red, white or
the prosecco bubbles.
My host noted the Holy Bible
propping the table. He spoke
briefly of schizophrenic disorders
common to many believers,
an image thing he said
they shared with their creator
and perhaps relevant
to himself as a young man
lacking a woman to relieve
his crisis of identity.
I found the food good
though not distinguished.
Table and chairs were of Italian design.
Money was scattered all about the floor,
I never got the dope as to why,
mostly yen and American dollars.
The view through the windows
was laudable: sail- and speed-
boats on the lake, jetters
under a blue heaven.
Our servers were good-lookers
in stiletto heels, Nordic,
or so they appeared to me —
former Olympian medallists, we were told,
specializing in whitewater kayak.
archery, the shot put.

A man seated opposite me
said when not on vacation
he was a fireman in Sioux Falls.
The orchid geneticist on my right ate
only her salad. Vegetarian, unmarried
and not hoping to be. She
had a fine relationship with
someone very special back home
and was upset that her cell phone
did not function 'down here'.
Our host gave her his.
The woman to my left
had a grandmotherly look
despite her sharp attire and
deep voice.

Following lunch we took a tour
by double-decker bus of the salt flats,
of the seventy-million-acre animal preserve,
the Old Masters Lost Art Museum
in the historic section of town,
finishing up at the bicycle factory (cyclists
were everywhere, accompanied by blue dogs
in affirmation of old world principle).

Late afternoon found us playing badminton
on hotel grass. The fireman and his young
spouse, a Teleprompter, prevailing.

Evening skiing in nearby mountains
was available for those so inclined,
or we could join the Nordic women
on a pub crawl or catch a popular musical
just down the street. I had a manicure

at the local spa and got a devil tattoo
on my left buttock.

The early-morning flight back home
was delayed. There were the usual problems
with Immigration. Business or pleasure,
I was asked. One never knows
quite what to say. All of you truth merchants,
the official told me, ought to be hanged.

Next morning I was back on the job at nine.
Truth had piled up quite a bit
during my absence. God knows
where it all comes from, or what
happens to it once it leaves my desk.

Leon Rooke is the irrepressible author of six novels and more than a dozen story collections. His novel *Shakespeare's Dog* (1983) won the Governor General's Award and his next novel, *A Good Baby*, was recently made into a feature film. A native of North Carolina, Rooke currently lives in the Annex area of Toronto with his wife Constance, and continues his long-time role as artistic director of the Eden Mills Writers' Festival.

———————

The author photograph was taken by John Haney and originally appeared on the cover of *The New Quarterly*, #86 (Spring 2004).